3-96

RAIN FOREST

by Ting and Neil Morris

Illustrated by Gillian Hulse

FRANKLIN WATTS
NEW YORK/CHICAGO/LONDON/TORONTO/SYDNEY

This symbol appears on some pages throughout this book. It indicates that adult supervision is advisable for that activity.

Franklin Watts
95 Madison Avenue
New York, NY 10016

Library of Congress Cataloging-in-Publication Data
  Rain forest / by Ting and Neil Morris.
      p. cm. — (Sticky fingers)
  Includes bibliographical references and index.
  Summary: Introduces the peoples, animals, and plants of the world's rain forests through a variety of easy-to-assemble projects made from simple household items.
    ISBN 0-531-14281-7
    1. Handicraft—Juvenile literature. 2. Rain forests—Juvenile literature. 3. Rain forest ecology—Juvenile literature. [1. Rain forest ecology. 2. Ecology. 3. Handicraft.] I. Morris, Neil.
II. Title. III. Series: Morris, Ting. Sticky fingers.
TT160.M663 1994
574.5'2642'0913—dc20   93-26686
                                              CIP   AC

Editor: Hazel Poole
Consultant: Simone Lefolii
Designer: Sally Boothroyd
Photography: John Butcher
Artwork: Gillian Hulse
Models: Emma Morris
Picture research: Juliet Duff

Printed in Malaysia

10 9 8 7 6 5 4 3

Contents

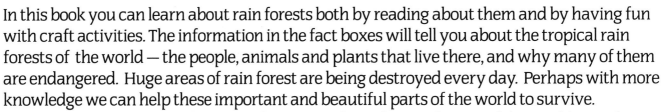

Introduction

In this book you can learn about rain forests both by reading about them and by having fun with craft activities. The information in the fact boxes will tell you about the tropical rain forests of the world — the people, animals and plants that live there, and why many of them are endangered. Huge areas of rain forest are being destroyed every day. Perhaps with more knowledge we can help these important and beautiful parts of the world to survive.

At the end of the book is a map to show you where the rain forests of the world are. There are also lists of books to read, places to visit, and organizations to contact if you want to find out more.

Now get ready to get your fingers sticky — making models and growing tropical things as you read about tropical rain forests.

Equipment and materials

The projects in this book provide an introduction to the use of different art and craft media, and need little adult help. Most of the objects are made with throwaway household "junk" such as boxes, plastic bottles and containers, newspaper, and fabric remnants. Natural things such as seeds, sticks, sand, and stones are also used. Paints, brushes, glues, and modeling materials will have to be bought, but if stored correctly will last for a long time and for many more craft activities.

In this book the following materials are used:

air-hardening clay
apple
balloons (long)
beads (small)
brushes (for glue and paint)
buttons
cardboard boxes (large and small)
charcoal (optional)
coins
cookie sheet
cotton spool
cotton thread
craft knife
cup
dowel rods
egg cartons
elastic
fabric scraps
felt -tip pens
felt scraps
flour
flowerpots
fork (old)
gardening wire
glue (water-based PVA, which can be used for thickening paint and as a varnish; glue stick)

gravel
jar (for mixing paint and paste)
knife
leaves
lemon
liquid detergent
matchsticks (used)
modeling clay
moss
needle (darning)
orange
paint (powder, ready-mixed, or poster paints)
paper (thick and thin cardboard; thin white paper; crêpe paper; corrugated paper; lining paper; cardboard; shiny paper; newspaper; tissue paper; construction paper)
paper bag (large)
paper doily
pasta shapes
pencils
picture hooks
pineapple
pipe cleaners
plant labels
plants (fern, ivy, moss; African violet [optional])
plastic bags
plastic bottle (large)

popsicle sticks
potting compost
ribbon
rolling pin
ruler
safety pins
salt
sand
scissors
seed trays
seeds (sunflower, melon, pumpkin, apple pips)
sequins (black)
sponge
spoon
sticks (long)
stockings
stones (small)
straws
tape (sticky tape; parcel tape; foil and colored tape)
teaspoon (old)
toothpicks
tree bark
twigs
varnish (PVA mixed with cold water)
wallpaper paste (fungicide free)
water
wax crayons
yogurt containers

Amazon Village

You can build your own rain forest village, with the smaller, family huts in a big circle around the larger, men's hut.

YOU WILL NEED:
- ✔ 5 egg cartons ✔ newspaper ✔ corrugated paper ✔ flour
- ✔ small cardboard box ✔ large cardboard base ✔ sand ✔ salt
- ✔ green and brown powder paints ✔ colored tissue paper
- ✔ green, brown, and yellow ready-mixed paints ✔ tape
- ✔ green crêpe paper ✔ PVA glue ✔ green construction paper
- ✔ modeling clay ✔ water ✔ craft knife ✔ scissors ✔ cup
- ✔ jar ✔ brushes (for glue and paint)

1 Use PVA glue to stick the cardboard box to the middle of the cardboard base. Then cut the tops off five egg cartons and stick them in a circle around the box.

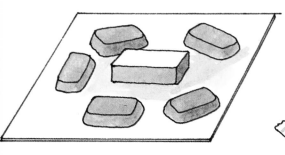

2 Mix a cup of flour with some water to make a smooth creamy paste. Cut up some newspaper into thin strips. Paste three layers of paper over the boxes. Let them dry.

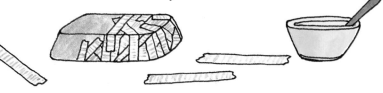

3 Ask an adult to cut a doorway into each hut with a craft knife. Paint the huts brown and yellow to look like thatched reeds.

4 This village is in a clearing, surrounded by rain forest. For tall trees, roll pieces of corrugated paper into tubes and tape them. Cut some leaves from green construction paper and glue them inside the top of the trunks. Make clusters of colorful fruit from crumpled-up tissue paper and stick them to the trunks. Make four cuts into the base of the trunks for roots. Fold the roots out and tape the trees onto the cardboard base.

5 You can make smaller trees using rolled-up sheets of paper, fringing and fanning out the tops for branches. Snip and turn out the bottoms for roots, then paint them and glue them down. For climbing vines, wind twisted strips of crêpe paper around the tree trunks.

6 Mix some fine sand or salt with green powder paint to make the forest floor. You can use plain sand for the clearing, or mix some salt with brown powder paint. Paint the cardboard base with glue and sprinkle it with the sand or salt.

Why not add some clay people to the village and animals to the forest?

People of the Amazon rain forest

The world's biggest tropical rain forest is in Brazil, South America. Here the Amazon River, the second longest river in the world, runs through the hot, steamy forest. It is thought that when Columbus reached America 500 years ago, at least six million Indians lived in the Amazon region. About 150,000 Amazonian Indians live in Brazil today. Some live in thatched reed houses, growing crops and hunting animals. Others collect latex from wild rubber trees to exchange for goods. But life is becoming harder and harder for these people, as large parts of the rain forest are being burned or bulldozed to the ground. It is estimated that over 116 square miles (300 square km) disappear every day. If this is allowed to continue, the Amazon rain forest could be gone by the year 2025.

Bird of Paradise

YOU WILL NEED:
- ✔ large cardboard base ✔ thick cardboard ✔ PVA glue
- ✔ jars ✔ blue and green powder paints ✔ glue stick
- ✔ yellow and white tissue and crêpe paper ✔ spoon
- ✔ large white, red, yellow, and orange wax crayons
- ✔ colored sticky tape ✔ buttons ✔ water ✔ scissors
- ✔ brushes (for glue and paint) ✔ bark ✔ stones ✔ coins
- ✔ corrugated paper ✔ paper doilies ✔ liquid detergent
- ✔ picture hook ✔ black shiny paper ✔ thin white paper

1 First make a rain forest background. Mix two spoonfuls of green powder paint with one spoonful of liquid detergent. Then mix one spoonful of blue powder paint with two spoonfuls of PVA glue diluted with cold water.

2 To make a comb for painting patterns, cut a zigzag edge along a piece of stiff cardboard, 4 x 6 inches (10 x 15 cm).

3 Brush some of the paint onto the cardboard base. Make twisting patterns with the comb, mixing the colors up. Then leave the background to dry.

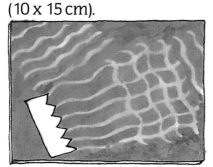

4 The bird's beautiful feathers are made from a collection of wax crayon rubbings. Make a collection of objects with various textures — bark, stones, coins, paper doilies, corrugated paper, and so on. Lay the white paper over each chosen object and rub the paper with the side of a wax crayon. Make some rubbings with the red crayon and then with the yellow.

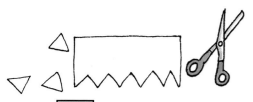

5 Cut your patterned paper into feather shapes.

6 Copy the outline of this bird of paradise on the rain forest background with white crayon.

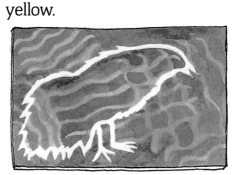

7 Tear some yellow paper into small pieces for the bird's head. Arrange the feather shapes and then glue them onto the picture as shown. Use some crumpled-up black tissue paper for the throat.

8 Cut some long strips of crêpe and tissue paper for the wonderful tail. Fringe the ends before gluing the tail on.

9 Add a beak made from shiny black paper, a button eye, and paint on two feet.

10 Stick some colored tape all around the edge, attach a picture hook to the back, and then hang your beautiful picture up.

Colorful rain forest birds

The beautiful bird of paradise lives in the rain forests of New Guinea and neighboring islands. The male bird has brilliantly colored plumage, which he shows off in courtship displays to attract female birds. The males, or cocks, of many other forest birds, such as the quetzal, cock-of-the-rock, peacock pheasant, and hummingbird, display very colorful feathers. Yet the female birds, or hens, often have rather dull plumage. The hens spend a lot of time in the nest sitting on their eggs and their dull appearance makes them less noticeable to animals which would otherwise try to attack them. The little hummingbird has a very long thin bill for probing into tropical flowers to feed on nectar. Its wings vibrate very rapidly so that it can hover and even fly backward, and this vibration produces the humming noise that gives the bird its name.

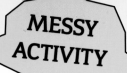

Growing Tropical Plants

You can grow your own indoor tropical forest.

YOU WILL NEED:
- ✓ potting compost ✓ orange
- ✓ lemon ✓ pineapple ✓ knife
- ✓ yogurt containers ✓ water
- ✓ plastic bags ✓ seed trays
- ✓ plant labels ✓ flowerpots
- ✓ gravel or broken pot

!

1 Cut an orange and a lemon in half and take out some pips. Soak the pips in two yogurt containers for 24 hours before planting.

2 Fill two seed trays with compost and water them to make the compost moist. Then plant the orange pips in one tray and the lemon in the other, pushing them about 1/2 inch (1 cm) into the compost.

3 Keep the trays in a warm place and make sure that the soil is always kept moist. Now you have to be patient — it will take up to three or four weeks for seedlings to appear. When the seedlings are large enough to handle, with about six leaves each, replant the strongest-looking plants into separate pots filled with potting compost. Your orange and lemon trees will grow best in a light and sunny room at a temperature of 65 – 75°F (18 – 24°C).

4 Complete your indoor forest with a beautiful pineapple plant. First ask an adult to cut the spiky top off a pineapple, leaving about 1 inch (3 cm) of fruit attached. Leave this to dry for 12 hours.

5 Put some gravel or bits of broken pot over the holes in a flowerpot, fill the pot with moist compost, and plant the pineapple top in it.

6 Cover the pot with a plastic bag. and keep it on a sunny window sill. When new leaves start growing from the pineapple, remove the bag.

Trees and plants

In tropical rain forests it rains nearly every day of the year, and it is always warm. Because of this climate, plants grow all year around and are always green. There are many different kinds of trees in the rain forest. Large numbers of trees tower to a height of over 200 feet (60 m), and the green foliage of their branches and treetops spread out like a huge umbrella — called a canopy — to shade the forest floor. Many big trees have large roots spreading out from the base of the trunk. These help the trees stand when tropical gales lash the canopy. Big trees also support smaller plants, called epiphytes, that grow on them. Epiphytes, such as orchids, ferns, bromeliads, and even cacti, do not kill their hosts. Large vines called lianas climb up the trees to get to sunlight, and they help to knit the canopy together. Some lianas kill the tree they live on.

Label all your plants and keep them moist and warm. Although you will probably not be able to harvest the fruits of your forest, it will be fun watching them grow.

Feather Headdress

On special occasions, the rain forest men of New Guinea wear headdresses made from the beautiful feathers of the bird of paradise.

YOU WILL NEED:
✓ corrugated paper   ✓ straws
✓ brown, red, yellow, white, and green tissue paper   ✓ glue
✓ parcel tape   ✓ scissors
✓ ruler

1 For the headband, cut a strip of corrugated paper 21½ x 2½ inches (55 x 6 cm). Fit the strip around your head and stick the ends together with parcel tape.

2 Tear some brown, red, green, and yellow tissue paper into small pieces. Screw them up and glue them to the outside of

3 Cut out some feathers, about 7 inches (18 cm) long, from pieces of brown, yellow, red, and white tissue paper.

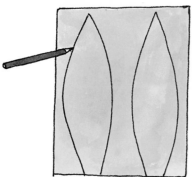

4 Glue the feathers onto thin plastic straws, leaving about 1½ inches (4 cm) at the bottom end of each straw. Then fringe the feathers as shown. Make some small feathers as well, using straws that have been cut in half.

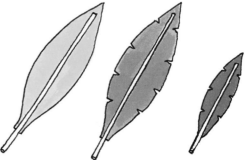

5 Slot the ends of the long straws into the holes in the paper on the top of the headband.

6 Push the smaller feathers into the holes at the bottom. Your headdress is now ready to wear.

Birds of paradise are now quite rare, as their feathers were in great demand. But you can enjoy wearing your tissue-paper headdress — it's environmentally friendly!

New Guinea and Australia

The region of southeast Asia is hot and wet all year around, and much of it is covered by tropical rain forest. The forests throughout this region contain valuable wood such as teak and mahogany. New Guinea, at the eastern end of the region, lies just north of Australia. The lower areas of this large island are covered with thick rain forest. Here there are known to be 251 different types of trees that give edible fruit. But the forests are disappearing, as many more trees are being cut down than are planted for the future.

Most of Australia is very dry, but there are rain forests near the northeastern coast. In places, the forest grows right down to the beach, which makes it very popular with tourists. It contains a canopy of eucalyptus, silky oak, kauri, red cedar, and Queensland teak. Rainforest areas here are now national parks.

Jungle Jewelry

Rain-forest people decorate themselves with shells, leaves, seeds, fur, claws, and bones. Our jewelry here looks similar, but is made of different things.

YOU WILL NEED:
- ✔ pasta shapes — large and small macaroni, wheels and whirls
- ✔ ribbon ✔ cardboard ✔ red, blue, black, and yellow felt-tip pens
- ✔ elastic ✔ PVA glue ✔ apple pips ✔ tape ✔ poster paint
- ✔ sunflower, melon, and pumpkin seeds ✔ scissors ✔ ruler
- ✔ varnish ✔ brushes (for glue and paint) ✔ cookie sheet

1 Use felt-tip pens to color the macaroni red, blue, black, and yellow.

2 Color the other pasta shapes with poster paints. Wait for the paint to dry and then varnish the shapes.

3 When the shapes are dry, thread them onto about 40 inches (1 m) of ribbon. To make the pasta beads hang down at the front, thread the ribbon through a large piece of macaroni, then through another pasta shape, and back through the macaroni. You can vary the design by going through a number of pasta shapes before going back through the first shape.

4 Try the necklace on for size, and tie the ends with a double knot.

5 Make a matching headband. When you have threaded the beads onto the ribbon, tie it with a bow around your head.

6 For a bracelet, cut out five 1½ x 2-inch (3 x 5 cm) shapes from cardboard.

7 Brush some glue onto the cardboard shapes, and press seeds and pips into the glue. Fresh melon and pumpkin seeds can be dried on a cookie sheet in a slow oven before use. Ask an adult to help you.

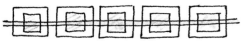

8 When the glue has dried, turn the decorated shapes over and arrange them in a row. Place a piece of elastic 8½ inches (22 cm) long in the middle and attach it with 1½-inch (3-cm) pieces of tape.

9 Tie the ends with a double knot and slip the bracelet over your arm or leg.

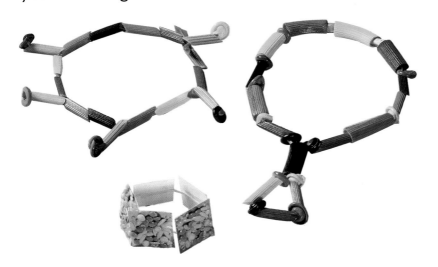

Mbuti 'Pygmies'

The Mbuti are a group of rain forest people found mostly in the Ituri forest of Zaïre, in the heart of Africa. They were the first people to come to this region. They are slight in build and are the shortest people in the world. The average adult man is only about 55 inches (140 cm) in height. They hunt animals such as monkeys and deer, and gather roots, fruit, and nuts as they wander through the forest, building new huts as they go. Their weapons are bows and poison arrows, spears, and blowpipes. They also climb tall trees to gather honey from wild bees' nests. The Mbuti worship nature spirits and look on the forest as the giver of all life.

Jaguar Disguise

1 Find a large, strong paper bag which fits loosely over your head and sits on your shoulders. Now ask an adult to mark the position of your eyes. Then take the bag off and cut out two small eye holes.

YOU WILL NEED:
- ✔ large strong paper bag (without handles)
- ✔ thick white paper
- ✔ flour ✔ black felt
  - or paper for stuffing
- ✔ glue stick ✔ brushes
- ✔ safety pin ✔ scissors
- ✔ 8 pipe cleaners
- ✔ green and black construction paper
- ✔ old stocking or tights, and fabric scraps
- ✔ pencil ✔ yellow ready-mixed paint
- ✔ black and brown poster paints
- ✔ spoon ✔ yogurt container

2 For the ears, copy this shape onto a piece of thick paper 3 x 4 1/2 inches (8 x 12 cm). Leave a 3/4-inch (2-cm) fold at the bottom and cut out two ears.

3 Fill a yogurt container with yellow ready-mixed paint, thicken it with a spoonful of flour, and then mix in a little brown paint. Brush this thick mixture onto the bag and ears with big strokes.

4 When the paint is dry, fold the ears and glue them to the top of the bag.

5 Cut out two green circles, 2 1/2 inches (7 cm) across. Bend each circle in half and cut a small semicircle out of the fold. Then glue the green circles over the eye holes in the bag.

6 To make a nose, cut an 3 1/4-inch (8-cm) square out of black paper, and then cut the square in half diagonally. Round off the corners of one triangle and glue the black nose on the head.

7 Add some jaguar's spots with black poster paint. Outline the eyes with black paint too, and add a friendly mouth.

Big cats of the rain forest

A leopard is smaller than a lion or tiger, but it is perhaps the fiercest cat of all. Unlike most big cats, the leopard is a skillful climber. It lives in Africa and southern Asia. A leopard will often lie quietly on a branch in the forest, waiting to spring on its prey. This might be an unsuspecting chimpanzee, or a small monkey. In South American rain forests, the brightly spotted jaguar, which looks like a slightly bigger leopard, rules from forest floor to canopy. It is the deadly enemy of other animals, eating deer, tapir, peccary, fish, and even alligator. Jaguars are expert swimmers and fishers. They will sometimes lie on a branch over a pool or river and scoop fish out of the water with their sharp claws.

8 When the spots are dry, stick some pipe-cleaner whiskers on each side of the mouth.

9 Your jaguar's tail is a stocking stuffed with soft paper or fabric scraps. Then cut out lots of black felt dots and glue them on. Close the open end of the stocking with a safety pin.

Now put on your mask, pin on your tail, and go on the prowl!

Clay Creepy-Crawlies

1 Worms
Roll a small lump of clay into a thin worm. Make some short and some long worms. Mark segments with a toothpick, and let the worms dry in a wriggly shape.

YOU WILL NEED:
✔air-hardening clay ✔thin gardening wire ✔matchsticks
✔pink tissue paper ✔toothpicks ✔poster paints
✔varnish ✔PVA glue ✔knife ✔brushes ✔sponge
✔pipe cleaners ✔10 small beads ✔leaves ✔twigs
✔stones ✔moss ✔scissors ✔water

2 Snails
Roll out a fat clay sausage and then cut it into two stumpy snail bodies. Shape a head and a tail. To make a shell, roll a thin clay sausage around and around and stick it on the snail's body. Use a wet sponge to moisten the join. Of course, you could use a real empty snail's shell, if you can find one in your garden! Use two used matchstick ends for horns, and push them into the soft clay.

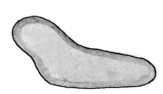

3 Centipede
The centipede has a long clay body marked with segments. Cut short lengths of gardening wire to make legs, and push a length through each segment, bending the wire to look like feet. Centipedes have a pair of legs on each segment, and at least 15 segments. How many legs does your centipede have?

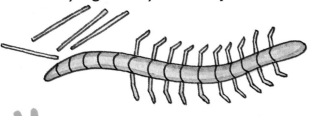

4 Spider
Mold a spider's body and head from clay. Press some tiny beads into the head for eyes (spiders have eight!). Push four pipe cleaners through the body to make eight legs, and stand the spider up. Press small lumps of clay firmly around the pipe cleaners.

5 Butterfly

Roll out a ball of clay and shape it to make the body. Bend some thin wire into two wing shapes, and then glue pieces of tissue paper over the wire. Cut away the extra tissue paper, push the wings into the body, and add two wire feelers.

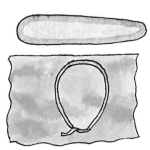
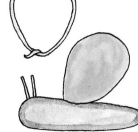

6 Snake

Roll out a long clay sausage and mold it into a snake. Press two beads into the head for eyes and cut a mouth. Use a toothpick to mark the snake's skin with V-shapes.

Insects, arachnids, and reptiles

The rain forest makes a wonderful home for insects. The world's largest beetle lives in the tropical forests of Africa. This is the goliath beetle, which grows up to 6 inches (15 cm) long and weighs up to $3^1/2$ ounces (100 g). Its gray-brown coloring helps it to hide among dead leaves on the forest floor. The biggest arachnid, the goliath bird-eating spider, lives in the coastal rain forests of South America. It can have a leg span of up to 11 inches (28 cm)! Many mosquitoes carry malaria, and both the disease and treatment come from the rain forest. Malaria can be treated with quinine, from the bark of the cinchona tree. Many snakes, such as the emerald tree boa, live in the rain forest too. The anaconda likes trees near water. This huge snake grows up to 30 feet (10 m) long. It drags its prey, a mammal or a bird, underwater and squeezes it to death.

7

Leave all the clay creepy-crawlies to dry for a day or two before painting them in bright colors. Wait for each coat of paint to dry before adding another color on top. When the creatures are dry, varnish them.

You could make an arrangement of leaves, twigs, and moss for your creepy-crawlies to hide in.

Lolly-stick Stilt Hut

YOU WILL NEED:
- ✔ packet of flat popsicle sticks (about 30 sticks)
- ✔ 14 dowel rods or sticks (about 8 inchers (20 cm) long)
- ✔ 8 bendy twigs or pipe cleaners
- ✔ leaves
- ✔ air-hardening clay or modeling clay
- ✔ rolling pin
- ✔ gardening wire
- ✔ thread
- ✔ PVA glue
- ✔ brush
- ✔ ruler
- ✔ scissors

1 First make a flat forest floor to build the hut on. Roll a lump of clay into a 6 x 10 inch (15 x 25 cm) sheet, about ¹/₂ inch (1 cm) thick.

2 Mark out the dimensions of the hut. It is approximately 3¹/₂ x 8¹/₂ inches (9 x 22 cm). The long sides are made up of six dowel rods. Stick the rods into the clay about ³/₄ inch (2 cm) from the edge. Place them 1 inch (3 cm) apart and firm each one down with a bit more clay. When one side is complete, stick the other six rods opposite them, leaving a 3¹/₂ inch (9-cm) gap.

3 Complete the stilts by sticking a rod in the middle of each short side.

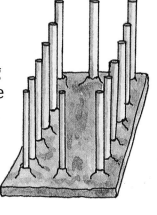

4 Build the platform floor about 2³/₄ inches (7 cm) above the ground. Weave two bendy twigs around the rods on all four sides, as shown. If you can't find any bendy twigs, use pipe cleaners, twisting two together to make longer ones.

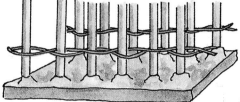

5 Tie the ends together at the corners with a piece of gardening wire. Ask an adult to help you cut the wire.

6 Now make the floor with popsicle sticks. Place them side by side across the width of the hut, pushing the ends between the intertwined twigs. Three sticks should fit between two rods.

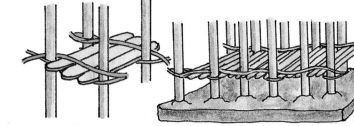

7 The roof is made in the same way as the floor. Leave a 3-inch (8-cm) gap between the floor and the roof supports. Weave twigs around the rods as you did for the floor. Place another layer of popsicle sticks across the width of the hut.

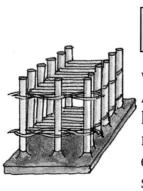

8 Paint the sticks with PVA glue and cover them with lots of strong leaves. Add several layers of leaves to make a thick roof. Paint the back of each leaf with glue before sticking it down.

9 Now all you need is a ladder for people to climb into the stilt hut. Make the ladder with two long and two short twigs, tied together with thread.

Rain forest huts

The Negritos live in small family groups in the rain forests of Malaysia, the Philippines, Indonesia, and New Guinea. They are similar to the African "Pygmies" and are less than 5 feet (1.5 m) tall. All their food and other needs come from the forest. They collect fruits, roots, nuts, and shoots. Monkeys, lizards, snakes, and birds are hunted with long bows and poison arrows, and fish are caught with spears. But they do not usually stay in one place for long. When they have eaten all the food in one part of the forest, they move on. Sometimes they build huts on stilts, to raise them up from the damp forest floor. They make a framework of thin branches and a roof of thatched leaves. The Dayak people of Borneo live in big wooden longhouses, also built on stilts. As many as 50 families may live in one longhouse.

Miniature Tropical Garden

MESSY ACTIVITY

1 Cut the bottle carefully — about a quarter of the way down from the neck — so that the top can be fitted over the bottom. You may need an adult to help.

YOU WILL NEED:
- ✔ clear plastic drink bottle ✔ old fork
- ✔ gravel or washed pebbles ✔ cotton spool
- ✔ potting compost ✔ charcoal (optional)
- ✔ selection of plants, perhaps including moss, fern, ivy, and African violet (optional)
- ✔ old teaspoon ✔ tape ✔ spoon
- ✔ scissors ✔ long sticks ✔ water

2 Spoon a layer of gravel or washed pebbles about 1¹/₂ inches (4 cm) deep into the bottom of your bottle. Then add a thin layer of crushed charcoal, which is good for drainage and keeps the bottle garden clean.

3 Cover the gravel and charcoal with 2¹/₂-3 inches (6-8 cm) of soil.

4 You will need a set of miniature garden tools. Attach long sticks to an old fork and teaspoon with tape. A long stick pushed into a cotton spool can be used for firming down soil.

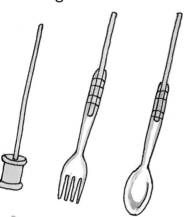

5 Look at your selection of plants. The taller ones are best placed in the middle or at the back of the bottle. Scoop a small hole with the spoon and lower the first plant into it, using the fork and spoon as shown.

6 Cover the roots with soil and firm down with the cotton spool. Add more plants in the same way, making shallow holes for clumps of moss.

7 When your tropical garden is complete, trickle some water down the inside of the bottle.

8 Put the cut-off part of the bottle over the garden and secure it with tape. If drops of water form on the inside of the bottle, take the lid off until they have evaporated. With the lid on, the plants in your miniature garden will grow without much watering.

9 Spray the garden with water occasionally to keep the soil moist. Keep the bottle in a light place, but not in direct sunlight.

See how quickly your garden grows!

Tropical climate

Tropical rain forests grow where it is hot and wet. The average temperature is at least 75°F (24°C), and tropical rain forests receive about 90 inches (230 cm) of rain each year. The climate never changes much in the tropics — the area of the Earth's surface near the equator. Here there are no seasons and most days in the forest are the same. After sunrise, the early-morning mists soon disappear. Warm, moist air rises as the wet forest is warmed by the sun. This forms clouds and by the afternoon there is usually a heavy rainstorm. It gets cooler at night. Tropical rain forests have the greatest variety of plants, and among these is the biggest flower in the world, the rafflesia. This plant is a parasite that grows on the roots of other plants. It has a smell of rotten meat and its flower can measure up to 3 feet (90 cm) across!

Forest Festival

1 To make and dress up a forest friend, first put a large sheet of paper on the floor. Ask a friend to lie down on the paper. Then draw around your friend with a pencil. Put another piece of paper down, for your friend to draw around you.

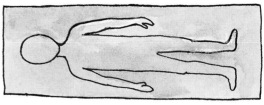

2 Cut out the shapes. Then cut out some eyes, a nose and a mouth from construction paper and stick them on your shapes.

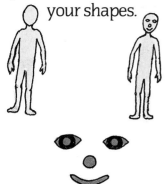

3 Cut some strips of tissue paper and arrange them on the head in an interesting hairstyle before gluing them down.

4 Cut out some tissue paper leaf and feather shapes, and make them into clothes and headdresses for your forest friends.

5 Mix some poster paint into red earth colors and paint the faces and bodies with it. When this is dry, add some colorful patterns to the faces and bodies. Outline the eyes with black paint.

6 For their festival, the forest people wear lots of beads. You could make some jungle jewelry as shown on pages 14–15, or you can decorate your friends with paper chains. Cut some colored construction paper into strips 3/4 inch (2 cm) wide. Then cut each strip into pieces about 3 inches (8 cm) long.

7 Roll one strip into a ring and glue the edges together. Loop a second strip through the ring and glue it. Carry on in this way until the chain is long enough to fit around the paper people.

8 Snakes belong to the forest, and your forest friends are not afraid to put a snake around their neck. Our snake streamer is made of long strips of paper 1½-inch (4-cm) wide. Stick two strips together like this, then start folding as shown.

9 Always fold the bottom strip over the top one. When you come to the end of two strips, add two new strips and carry on until the snake is long enough. Draw on some eyes and a mouth, and then wind the snake around one of your forest friends.

Face and body paints

Many rain-forest peoples paint their faces and bodies and decorate themselves with jewelry. Usually they do this on religious festival days. The people of the New Guinea highlands are famous for their amazing dress and makeup. They paint their faces and bodies in strong colors which they make from earth. The patterns they paint are connected to religious beliefs and superstitions. The men of some tribes wear mud masks, which give them a very frightening appearance. They also wear magnificent headdresses.

Scientists have learned a lot from rain-forest people about plants that are useful to our industrial society. For example, gums and resins that ooze from rain-forest trees give us some of our commercial paints and dyes.

Now let the festival begin!

Flying Toucan

1 Blow the balloon up to about 1 foot (30 cm) in length and tie it with a knot. Then carefully wind some string around the balloon, to make a head and body shape.

YOU WILL NEED:
- long balloon
- thin gardening wire
- black sequins or sticky spots
- ruler
- wallpaper paste (fungicide-free)
- scissors
- white, yellow, and black ready-mixed paint
- PVA glue
- blue and red poster paints
- 2 large buttons
- string
- newspaper
- darning needle
- pencil
- tape
- black tissue paper
- cotton thread
- thick cardboard
- brushes (for glue and paint)
- black tissue paper

2 Cut out two wings from thick cardboard, about 4 x 6 inches (10 x 15 cm). Wind some wire around the wings.

3 For the top half of the beak, fold a 5 x 7 inch (12 x 18 cm) piece of cardboard in half, draw this shape and cut it out. Then make the bottom half of the beak in the same way, but 1/2 inch (1 cm) narrower on each side and 1 inch (3 cm) shorter.

4 Attach the two halves of the beak to the balloon with tape.

5 Tear some newspaper up into thin strips and small square pieces.

6 Mix the wallpaper paste according to the instructions on the packet, and paste the newspaper strips all over the balloon.

7 Paint the beak with wallpaper paste and cover both parts, inside and out, with newspaper pieces. Allow the beak and the body to dry.

8 Meanwhile spread the paste over a sheet of black tissue paper and wrap this around a wing. Wrap each wing in at least two sheets of tissue paper. Then wait for the wings to dry.

9 Cover the body with another two layers of paper strips and let it dry.

10 Now paint your toucan. First cover it with white paint. Wait for this to dry, and then paint the body black. Leave the chest and beak white.

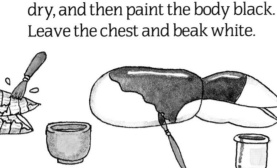

11 When this is dry, paint the white beak with thick yellow paint, and later add blue and red markings with poster paints. Glue on two button eyes.

12 Before attaching the wings to the toucan, add some black sticky spots. Then secure them with pieces of wire. Push the wire through the wings and in and out of the paper body.

13 Ask an adult to thread a needle and push it through the toucan's body. Then you can hang your toucan from the ceiling, to remind you of your journey through the rain forest.

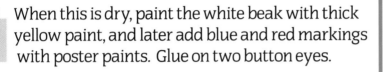

Toucans and parrots

Much of the plant food in rain forests is found high in the trees. Many rain-forest birds have developed special ways of getting their food. The toucan has an enormous beak that is sometimes as long as its body. It uses its brightly colored beak to reach fruits growing on thin branches. The sawlike edges make the beak even more effective. Toucans travel in flocks and are found in forests from Mexico to Argentina. Parrots and macaws have very powerful beaks, and both their upper and lower jaws can move. They use their beaks to crack open nuts and fruit stones. A parrot's tongue is strong too. It can curl around a nut to get it out of its shell. Parrots are also among the best climbing birds. Some use their beak as a third foot to pull themselves along a branch or up a tree trunk.

Tropical Rain Forests of the World

There are three main areas of tropical rain forest in the world. The largest is the South American forest around the Amazon River. This makes up over a third of the world's rain forest area. The other big areas are in central Africa and southeast Asia.

North America

Equator

Africa

South America

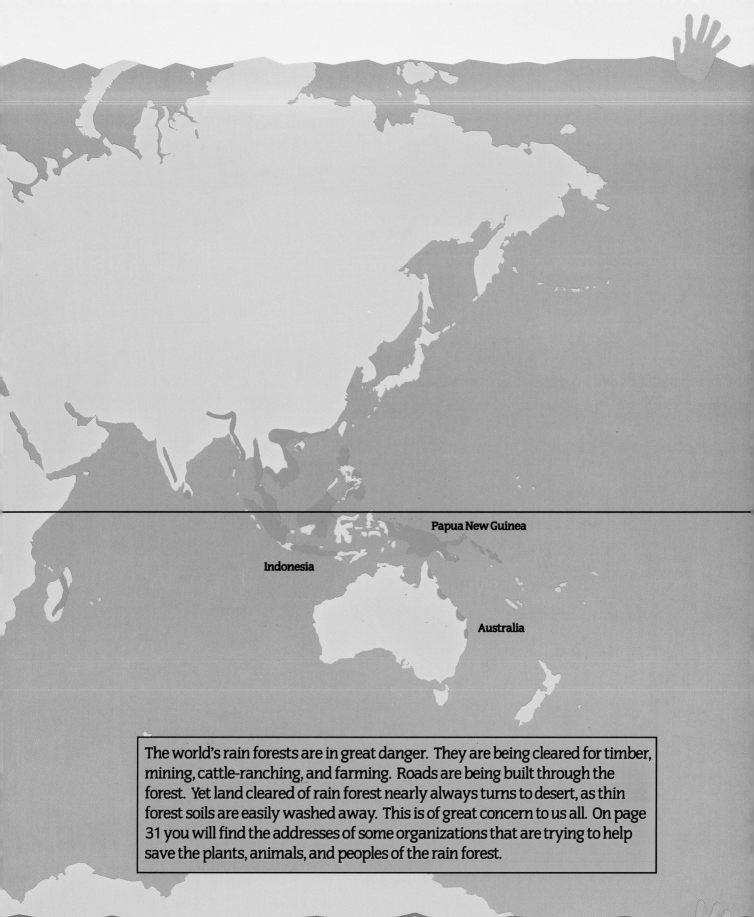

Papua New Guinea

Indonesia

Australia

The world's rain forests are in great danger. They are being cleared for timber, mining, cattle-ranching, and farming. Roads are being built through the forest. Yet land cleared of rain forest nearly always turns to desert, as thin forest soils are easily washed away. This is of great concern to us all. On page 31 you will find the addresses of some organizations that are trying to help save the plants, animals, and peoples of the rain forest.

Glossary

arachnids - a group of eight-legged animals that includes spiders and scorpions.

blowpipe - a long tube for shooting poisoned darts by blowing.

buttress roots - large roots that support the trunk of a tree.

canopy - the high level of most of the branches and leaves in a forest, forming a covering like an umbrella.

edible - fit to be eaten.

epiphyte - a plant that grows on another plant but does not feed on it.

flock - a group of birds.

hover - to stay in one place in the air.

latex - a milky fluid from the rubber tree, used to make rubber.

liana - a woody climbing plant.

longhouse - a long wooden house lived in by many families.

malaria - an infectious disease carried by mosquitoes.

mammal - a warm-blooded backboned animal whose young feed on their mother's milk.

national park - an important area of land that is protected and can be visited by the public.

nectar - a sugary fluid in plants.

parasite - a plant or an animal that lives on another (the host) and obtains food from it; the parasite is usually harmful to the host.

peccary - a piglike mammal.

plumage - a bird's feathers.

prey - an animal hunted by another animal for food.

quinine - a bitter substance extracted from the cinchona tree and used to help treat malaria.

rain forest - thick forest found in areas of heavy rainfall. Tropical rain forests are found near the equator. Temperate rain forests are found in temperate zones.

stilts - long posts used to support a building above ground level.

tropical - situated in the tropics, the hottest part of the Earth's surface near the equator.

Resources

Books to read

Rainforest by Rodney Aldis (New York: Macmillan Child Group, 1991)

Why are the Rain Forests Vanishing? by Isaac Asimov (Tulsa, Okla.: Gareth Stevens, Inc., 1992)

Life in the Rainforests by Lucy Baker (New York: Franklin Watts, 1990)

Tropical Rainforest by Michael Bright (New York: Gloucester Press, 1991)

Rainforest by Michael Chinery (New York: Random House, 1992)

One Day in the Tropical Rain Forest by Jean C. George (New York: Crowell Junior, 1990)

Rainforest Destruction by Tony Hare (New York: Franklin Watts, 1990)

Tropical Rain Forests Around the World by Elaine Landau (New York: Franklin Watts, 1991)

The Rainforest by Laura Tangley (New York: Chelsea House, 1992)

Places to visit

American Museum of Natural History
Central Park West and
    Seventy-ninth St.
New York, NY 10023

Chicago Natural History Museum
Roosevelt Road and
    Lakeshore Drive
Chicago, IL 60605

Smithsonian Institution
Museum of Natural History
Constitution Avenue at
    Tenth St., NW
Washington, D.C. 20560

Organizations to contact

Environmental Defense Fund
257 Park Avenue So.
New York, NY 10010

Greenpeace USA
1436 U St., NW
Washington, D.C. 20009

Rainforest Alliance
270 Lafayette St., Suite 512
New York, NY 10012

Sierra Club
730 Polk St.
San Francisco, CA 94109

World Wildlife Fund
1250 24th St., NW
Washington, D.C. 20037

Index

Additional Photographs:

Bruce Coleman (cover), 9, 17, 19, 23, 25; Zefa 3, 7, 11, 13, 15, 21, 27.